Scapes

Jessica Grim

SPUYTEN DUYVIL
New York City

ISBN 978-1-963908-18-3
Cover photo: Jessica Grim
Author photo: Nick Robinson
Library of Congress Control Number: 2024941241

For Alan, always; and for Sebastian
With thanks to Paula Morse,
for the space all those years ago, and the kindness

MIDWESTERN NOTES

SEASONS

SCAPES

END TIMES

MIDWESTERN NOTES

Concordance

The sewn binding
of the bibliographer
    an induction
ordered by history

     satellite of our desires to
cast ourselves   out
    under the shaking of
a voice   projected
      futures   keeping the word
close

clearing history of not
being able to see
the script   anymore

saturation point
from where we gaze   a
   kind of cloaking   from
within   which middle distance

a position bound w/in
the book
   sequence of un-named colors cascades
into the closed volume

we have seen it lurking
    in the foreshortened past
bereft of content
voided by a kind of
   nightly   hallowing

without ornament
to turn   the page

DAYBREAK

The size of obedience
retrograde emotion actually—
an egg rolls off the countertop

there is no more false dim than that of pre-dawn
world   as flatly present pastels

in which sky having more or less
fallen commits

in which the word falls
on the shadow of a hand writing

a tender fallacy
softly wearing away—
does that surprise

regarding the repository:
it is impossible to say
in what year it was conceptualized, in what
year the first entry, as it were, was made

The Field

    Across the plain curvature
retools to flat fields
  crops
    tipping across the gravel pit looking
for the rare   venom
      rumored
    to be there—
once again the landscape
righting   itself

  dusky notes
     fell
on   petals as they move
slightly   from the sound
  of their growing

Valley

Town sits on the   precipice
its tenses   correct
for how it sees itself

still view   written
on every surface

rearranged
       screed
  of the substratum

trains an eye
on the protocol
    sidling ache   greening
patches
showing through
    retrain toward spring

TILLAGE

In the farmlands' front yard
tender attempts to vocalize
in which the usual
fusion unglues

it's all sightline—
tolerated well
in the main

day's close blue—
slender branches move
        a most dependable
silence

microscopic lines connect you—
            pluralized, diurnal,
    flip-top, open frame to
the present
    thinking about
        trumpet vine revival—
            cod glue ruminant,
                cartilage
            a book explaining wind

a thousand provocations this
        rain falling
across   tillage

serviceable taxonomy
performs silhouette   silvery
        cicada hum   stops
garden mid-cry

practical entropy
    summers'   contusion
    green wall awash
tongue hold   demands elations

NOCTURNAL OTHERWISE

Hill in the distance hill   underfoot
contretemps in the cellar, allure awash
a name thrown down on
the table

redacted trauma—
the argument of the rain

cursive sound
recoils as atmosphere
        at night amplified
integers   connective
        acrimony
plateaus soften the
hand seen   in the dark

white dawn   array
  of grays & blues
tilted on the stem

protective flange
    approaching
        heedlessness a means
    by which we court
our   demise

the moment opening out as if
expectation was   itself
the thing
found   among the missing

lapsed signifiers
in the wild early fall

written as an end—
to a figuring nocturnal otherwise

Veritable Landscapes

1

Seraphim tinge—
near-interruption in nights' rain
        ordinary days   in various states
of strain or fray   on waking recites
a kind of macabre chant

could turn tornadic
        atmospheric stupor   northern
edge of southern storm never
mind those   torrents

former groves, glades, meadows, stands of
mixed deciduous trees
at the perimeter on
the perimeter road it is not
descriptive   enough

array of muted blues grays and mauves

temperate moraine   a
        misshapen   epic
which settles in a way which
        nothing
can
        settle

2

We who would welcome
the indeterminate soul back
among the breaches

a gelling of tendency
towards habit

roundness of light
a pause a hesitation
        gaze   lifts to reveal I
don't remember
what   it reveals

3

Appositional landscape
        at its edge
    our figurehead
trying to bring us   closer
below a bright sky

        emptiness filled and
with what   if you
imagine   going
east   from there

fully weighted barely
upright
        floating interior
    has   dimension when
    the plane turns you turn
in air

4

Dressed as themselves in
the dream so
as to recognize
themselves

      our singular
insularity the
same quiet snow
that   rubric of
      turns

5

Note of relief   rancid
among   rose petals   such
coloration   undoes
     attempts to cross
     a sequence but
without the rapture   normally attending
such   silver instructions

in the cold the tract which
     in the natural world would
result in brittleness
the crack of ice snap
of winter vines

a repetition the question
textured

multiplied by
sequencing,
          collapsing
light,   and the
interstices
this   early   twisting
     away

6

Sudden violent withering
    across
which snow lies in
      cold pages   ribs
on the roadside

     gardens' neglect the
pair founder   spring's
terrible indecision
    not yet budded   colors
infolded   upon
    themselves

The Want

This still scene wasn't

the dream of survival all but lost as they
became aware that the plane was becoming more
distant, not, as they had urgently hoped – and indeed
seen in their increasingly ragged delirium – moving
toward them   is not
        a sentence

to what extent does disruption adhere there –

somewhere else in the spectrum
I felt alone

confused by   continuing static
is that   static?

subtle ruination of the
surface's finish—
        knowing this
was an interesting condition—

these could otherwise have been
very different times
 – or that, in any case
was the myth
frying on the wind

literary memory voids
dream   of reading

why this curiosity this event

numerically atoned daybreak   aligns

this is the want

O2

The vision as time passes   becomes
fastened

forest gives way to fields which
give way to small towns, subdivisions,
industrial parks, suburban tracts and
finally the huge crater where once the city
itself had stood

the ground was in any
case   a reassurance

it was nearer the end
then

the character drawn slowly across
the page loses viability as ink
sprawls

signal perceptions
traces of commotion
its otherworldly
    softened curriculum

fantastical terracing
winds still
awash in waiting

OUR TENDER AGGRESSIONS

Withstand plummet –
    causeway
to take you from this world
to the next

test case   deluge
    the emblem   in which
destination   falters

mouth of the valley

effect of a simple line
        trees' tops at eye level

weight of the liquid against your lip
    light in a window
in sync w/the nation
naturally
       steadfast in its slide

border transgression
equal to   instilled myopia--
we were tirelessly wrong
   yet   it was
economical it   spoke
to our   senses

Memory 36

A wing a leaf how
quiet   its fixity
     running   against
          meaning

limb
bracken
follicle
seizure of desert lands

across the spectrum
     boundary trauma

low zone   addled
    epidemic of dementia
pasts as lived in dreams
     quietly
          verbs fall

lilt of the voice
all recall
in which one version varies so slightly
from the next

WHEN THERE

Shorefront tedium
        creasing and folding
  along   bifurcations
or   some other
   notifiable
 peace
        more like an interruption
in the calamity

dawns' purple brings
singularly   dark morning
   hand held out   just so

content sputters sidewalk
flops up to meet my
foot the aquatic "blip" of
        sound reduction
its   relationship
to memory

SEASONS

after *The journals of Lewis & Clark*

Year One

Spring I

As mooring
a colorful mix of
missteps the   search turning
out badly

May air gracing
uncollected sonorities

scattering of crowns
call it a counting ritual
    sum of their
            trappings

cool fugue, shady trope
apple blossoms
habituating as fast as they   can

wild loved ones
and the way the face had
of dissembling

SUMMER I

Anticipation of the
season tinged w/
a populated   nostalgia

sun's saturate   plots
as merciful as that a
roundness an angle

common scarcity
        loon's call
in   parched
    plots

acrid bright   of mid-day

they proceed apace
across the plain
cataloging   the ruminants

their sense of having been
rescued   intact

"up north" slow pools
of remorse   form
on the voyage
home

day spreads late
        summer glory
when looking down
        the daylight   intervenes
    the sureness
        of that
            anniversary

Fall I

A decision
   is no salve

clocking winter's approach

predisposition begins
with tedium where
were those
   thoughts   now   snow
bound
not   an absence of place
quite

    science   ungrounds
      washes
   against   us in the
horrible
      tide

such as having saved its color

some of whom were no longer
   living   others
    of whom   their
  mementos

Winter I

        Leaves retain color
after being removed
from the tree the red
  new snowfall
      on   ice

a series of removals
remedied   sky

salt of your life after
you've evaporated

reposition chronology
life's work   plows
   through
platinum anatomy

early foliage masks
edging where   you are
     not anymore

Year Two

SPRING II

Words flex
preposterously

    evening sound
      ratchets   a
fugue for   lordlessness
       chords' wager

    attributed on
       point   plant's form
   darkness   lakes' edge
    their having   landed
there

place   ornateness in
   morning sparing
         handedness not
evident
talking to each party
    in turn   the bloody
blossoms

Summer II

Thrown off by the maple
        – fledged or
flooded   terrain

        landscape that
descends   trestle
or   roadway crossing
      pacing   appears
luminous   storm deepened
    these roads   hold   down
      the lyric blend
of explosive
powders

so much
    setting out
winds squeeze birds'
cries   in its own words
    anything is news

FALL II

A form of wanting which
in delivering you back
to yourself   perpetually
writes   itself—

radial quiet   mid-day
    it was a good year
for the tree

scene on a river
this capacity then
this trenching
    waning of time against the lines
set   it

foundering notion of
coast   a carpet
of pronouns inking
      we, the lake their splintering
geography attracts

awaiting its clauses:
absence   the point
about the temperature—
causal blooming the
petals' shriveled attenuation

a palette the wide serif
trims   blurred fibrillation
lapped ending   intimates the
    hampering sunlight

Winter II

Incendiary snow sun
glows   weakly
    integers waiting to receive
        color

hoary frost   prevailing
      atomic circuitry
     depicting upon flat land and
the creases
    of the sky its cold

      the notebook contesting
definition
    the long night
an adoration
in its variance   its
buttes steppes and
turgid plains apparent

the weight of attrition
      in winter where we are

Year Three

Spring III

Natures' ambush
      arcs   held
surely marked by
a flattened fear an
imprecision
         as it were to
the plain

the serene act of the pasture
reshaped vertically
to dry

the surface words without
their   rapture

until our arrival the landscape
    no leaf should
shudder so

a leap
toward   spring—
      a cadence of silts

a melody which began to play
under the
new regime

where the night bends
the mock morning in its
darkness

as one is moving along-
side the river is
filtered such as
the light is there

Summer III

Calm   extinction
mid-century mist
as notes would indicate
they fled the troubles

spectral
      light falling   there is this
                  moment animating
time

in the wind there was
naturally   no plan to flower

one might inquire of
the prophetic nature
        of smallness   cutting
back invasive
            slippage
      attempt to get back
      sounds of
certain words
      wanting to know
            what is evident

Fall III

Against a background of
curious night

a clutch of bright yellow
in the low branches
of a single tree

line of differentiation   that
series of linkages, ridge tops, hollows

winter racing
against bodies
with its cold

low-flying emotive blips their
interrogation   our
home here

Winter III

Form the field took
astral trap   tampering
a   blueness
there   multiplied in the
hard atmosphere's late
     melts

interrogated moraine
a course of ruts & valleys
landing itself
a seasonal   blush

clotted skyline induces
scramble   looking forward
to lurching
     out of view again

SCAPES

Myopic

I am not so much attached to
my myopia as I am
hopelessly
in its sight

consequently, magenta
the trembling plan

softly blowing sea breeze sears

along the lower portion of the wall
air escapes in small gusts—

the floors, swept clear of sand,
are slightly vibrating

the sill   in question

remorse lacks   a little
punch

all flush lines lay down
here   and   here

Maui: A Western

Ocean threshold   billowy
black basalt along   green
            indigenous

quelling trend   temperate
swell form   in the ocean holding

single weed shoots up   not
dissimilar
      (in some way mortified)
   (seeking routine)
empire   surrogate

flattened seed pods' sheen
moderating reef   watch that
      bright spot
travel as
          recall

nouns' high heat
walls bloom as
          horizon
remotest archipelago on earth
cloud sarcophagus
          possibilities   only watching

a question of what
heat   can do
a curve   rivaling
itself for   beauty a
      well maintained system of
footpaths   eerie
   ʻaʻā flow

tiny   whitecaps attach
the thing to your
  ankle

COPP'S HILL

A confection
the well-formed windows
tell of a space

color at dusk   below us
positing   its sky
    what curvature

without print as a thirsting

cessation of sound   around the visitation
    river to the right dissembling

any hope of retrieval the
sorrel sound of histamine
        slow-walking   marching band
follows saint   on wheels

watched weather
come   east

test run
for loss of momentum
choreographed   epitome –
        glistening moment unusually
attended   across
the east or the
idea of what
east   was

a comportment a walking
        countenance   the word   to find
the river by which
included in the price of existing
you walk

a kernel to be found explaining
a phase of affliction

in summer slowly
describe increased warmth &
moisture   would seem
to indicate that building

pacing the city
was a child sentimentally
in the main, confused –
to glimpse its
reflection in the windows

a leaf fell in summer
still green and damp from the
afternoon's rain   and flew
against my neck   the cut
gutter stones of the walkway the
slanting stones
of the burying grounds

NYC

for Seb

We are trying to identify   how
we might – define again – perpendicular to
the ground the
elbows   elegantly

in its lack of stillness
a found symbol for stillness the
movement a rock
     stands   the path's
fringe collects the muss
          of those living   around it

orbit of the siren bird
this same   not seeing   so well
on the occasion of being
     the city   granting the scape

and of their concluding
          as particular—
the triumphant sighting
of a subterranean rat

Scottish Notes

Greenish gray
welds & vales rapeseed fields
painfully
     bright

imagining the sky another   color
everybody's geese   rotting
in the way that nothing   rots

tacitly subterranean
       under then under
       bin for body parts slated for loch
          lineage   balks
   parapet
   arms laying cheerily
       bustled up w/
themselves

sky hard upon town
  swivel-free
   against
      rock wall
anchored loft –
stains
  attributed to coal
  closes   a dream
of my swollen face

sun never properly
     set
keen
  to "see some mammals"
in The Minch, please

Speyside, Strathspey
   swells not really
to "prevent or treat" sickness some
patches show
    hope as a ferry   often
  does

DIXIE

Adaptability falters   over the
short grass of Alabama
every   leaf fell   sodden   the ground
filled   with   them

autumn sky divine   thin
limb encased evidence

hemisphere can hardly hold more
          dawn fissure
widened & paled word
parts wept

          sky-colored
arsenal   high winter sun
by then white
      threats   loosened
watching our weaker   anagrams
      test out
in the surrogate rush

search for meaning in
elevations
          flying
below the radar panoramically

cauterized empathy
interrogates   slight
shifting along a
line of indeterminacy

along the icy road   twin
velocities   speed

unspeakable aggression   winds
howl while   far away
missiles   fall   deftly
one wing drops
          just
    a little taste   which scans
      so   along the ear

St. Joe's Peninsula

I.

Air a scrim—
sounds' layers float
another sheet
     wafts in
   pine drops   a soft mat
an afternoon's
     elision

disabled waves' elevation
prescribes a kind of arrangement of the
trees   arcing out of barely
ruffled   water—   a school of
small silver fish

screens from which
we know another drifting
     the chance of waking   well

...how low in the sky
     the saltiness of waiting itself
that   scented abstraction

II.

Failure of clarity
     humidity   lowers
the possible limit of that
     cloud   blown over
figurines as it were
     dotting the shore

aerodynamics of noon   languor
     on the bay appearing
to comb for shells urchins dollar bills beaks
stems other stones fins sharks' teeth bits of floss tar
amber ingot feral gems...
     scree of cicadas   thunderheads
roll in over
partially scarped beach cusps

swash zone   wrack line
aeolian transport   patch of
     shell hash

regarding the sincerity or lack
of sincerity   of the shoals themselves
      crinkling along the edges

antonym frame for a guise no
calmness in sitting or   very little

Linwood Park I

Some landing   on
    the lake   as such   its
pasture rotting
     vari-colored plastics
along the breakwater

mapping our
gains   evidenced by
this perception of
green,   shades of sky the
    wind which
is a more or less steady
sound   in the configuring

writing through
the blind spot caused
by staring at the sun
     scraped
over the beach surface

it is or   was
    lapsed
a vessel its
slow speed suggests

sum of tides   zero

fading   white eye of   rock
as phrased
carbon angle   suppurating

            such wakes as they have
                    tiers
            collapse into
                    detritus

            pursed wind
            interminable lagoon

            water / sky
            line smudged then
            indiscernible

Linwood Park II

Exuberance leaching from
the landscape

    to gain
a clearer view
of the overcast

dark band at
horizon
    weather moving in   or out
husks   fall thickly
      how long
will you let those blossoms   lay

line lightens slightly and
spreads
studying the surface
    for felt or
imagined singularity
what claims the
"language encounter" makes

    sea or   lake worthy as
in some cases they were
    nearly   sailing there on the dark
   the surf
still slight
a fragile   recreation

Sonoran Notes

for Laurie

No   metaphor   there
      in the desert   morning
mica reflecting
   for instance a chemical breakdown
of that   wish

dawn's sounds
a frame for the body for
the landscape the sky against
spines   outcroppings the
trance the deliberate bird throws   an
            elevation   like so

forwardly down
the mtn as
expanse   endlessly not
stepped   off   into—

      from here a series of two dimensional
ridges rise sloping north

seepweed saguaro prickly pear—
yucca agave allthorn cholla—
      and other
      spears their sky
mine

is doubt a need a   single bloom, red, rises
the "secondary physics" of it
various greens
monocarpic, palo verde, ocotillo

END NOTES

END TIMES SONGS

I.

Late winter
sudden   still
    an enclosing
optimism
in the end times

hilarity of the silence
as often as not
and flatly
or more flatly than not

no more wild cold the
list of missing growing

swaying existence
of the species
    to be forgiven
until all forgiving
bodies   are gone

and that words
in the end
cannot do

necessity will pale
    and cannot, certainly
give that light

when shape of spring
intercedes a scent or ocular stream on
increasing velocity
of the currents

the ticking of the light

the kinds of birds they are,
too

II.

Arch   epileptic
    figure on elevated
T level autocrats carry
the day   simple   a pink sky

recreational breathing who
needs trees the lots
look sexier
as stubble you
have to admit

the littoral   notwithstanding

on account of our
pleasant natures
    & other   terrestrial
fictions

ocular pelt –
    floral screen fills
said brightness

did they ever
understand it

III.

Weight   of quotidian   penury
the last of the longest days' duration

platinate   silence
distanced gaze fidget
often seen as aerial our
domestic   canopy

spectral, enflighted, disastrous to
take up
where the water
left off

ritual would have
a word with them
when the season
rolls 'round

cheap assignation   hovers
   yellow day
      finds its color

privations of habit each
two after them
chase their earlier selves
an accurate reproduction
of a firmly held belief

wishes not falling lightly
as they should
on the plants' broad leaves but
beside them   somehow

it's the tilt
after all
    a kind of sanded down history
with which we line
our nest a dark figure
in flowing white
on a bright bluff and
nobody got
those light
light   eyes

IV

A deranging   sensibility
carpets   exterior plane as
you see   crossing itself out
of & away from
the land

in the regressive heat
of our dismay

lightly devastated
landscape lovely in
this light which is to say
the dark

how "relative" is thoughtfulness

everything about your
portal   became
          adversity   awaiting the unborn
tapping along spines
by feel to get there

hubris of noon transgresses
our decorative failures
profound under-
tow as in stripping
away language

A Dawn

As it is
not yet breaking

corrugated troubles
swarming bees in the cold
      imagined   as a cloud,
suspended btwn
quotations

where the dark
despite the date
the astounded credit
given

inert landscape bumps along
a seeking entity eluded the
antonym it sought

weird flames flatten the hedge
the wars were so close

Untitled (1)

genes
corrupting
the quenching

sequence
memory
some
version   of not a
care in the
crippling   aside
as sorrowful other

in the room
grown quiet in the
home   grown
quiet   the very
lapses   degrade
our   antipathies
toward reserve

if by mindful we meant
sweltering   wrong
hold then
careen   against
        useless in
the face of
as they had been
so long
in their silence

each slow note carrying
its weight
as a howling

the which way of integers
drifting by

birds steeping
in roof's
pitch

they were unusually
passing   fretting
on the open plains
of illness

signifier hunching away
from its signified

THE ROAD HOME

Child in green receding
into nearness you thought first of
as distance

moving sideways across
punitive tundra

forest trope against
mountain trope
plains trope steady
trope   of rain falling
standing man
in deer suit trope
neural captivity
trope

a season its anatomy
your friend,   the analysis
syllabics of the prism
same as the similar   self   in
falling or floating

molecules   freshening   the distance

wind rank   if birds had
different ways to fly which
they do
invidious wish
a calling occurred   near the
        epicenter   granular view
across shoals

being delivered   alone
with the view   the road
the real road
home

Bird Poem

During the flood this became
a sound often overheard

factualizing   truncation
something
unpeopled a tide a
signature   blank
holds steady

parsing sky
a western sensitivity to light
morning sun a tension
pilloried   in the town

trafficking in wildness and in
        coastal anticipation
wavery retribution   phlox
on a hill the pain in the chest it's
the samba   all over again

tincture rising
narrative stent

we cannot nor do we
do not

intention's tonalities
a ray, framed
slowly tanks composure

serrated season

all the tombs entwined
a scorched literal layering

with which singleness
self-same   arability

sighting the first cardinal
and an owl   I thought   in the bare
trees yesterday   ideas
twist in the wind   and cannot
adjust to the reality they find
themselves in

Untitled (2)

In late august
the fullness
drained of insect sound oddly
slow in
unusual   cool

spirit churns
interment
of dates & the
habitual   disinterment
of same

the conditions
of what

along the beaded line
days tick off
        violence   holding up
the horizon

our favorite
particulate   matter

as if violence
were individual
rather than
systemic I wait
for *these*   to die

The Tornado

Unlike common species
surrounding them
winds
never arrived
didn't come
across fields didn't
graze the sides of the house
in passing
even
    and for that they
were   thankful
a terror from a next life
overstepped

words
    adhere to
        basal linguistics
nominal instance
of defibrillated air
bumping up against
the   ear
    along streets
roads and boulevards the
sameness often
    visits

MEMORIAL DAY

for Walter Bernard

Utterances across
open planes collapse their
vortices pulling
them to dust

not so
much as in the past
the   audible echo
of sleep follows
the wait for dawn

tones of gold & orange
signify   warm south out
of reach in the antiseptic light

of all of our favorite names a
decision slows the mind   categories
of blame, serial imaginations

monument aggrieved
large porthole for humanity
floats up in
its vehicle arguing
with itself

fancy not keeping
a promise and the
void into which you
fall is not
so sudden as it seems

tiny crowd
on the far shore of the small creek
stands   and for each
war a flower

a brightening or
nearly a brightening

slowly into the small canyon
the morning sun so that
each   becomes legend

lavender mint rosemary star
jasmine   not   really
growable   in other
than this pitched   terrain

this question of blood
relations as we are
so   few

connections brittle spun
of thinnest   circumstance

Dream No. 2

In which I am both in and am viewing
a landing   in green fields
a barn in the near distance behind
which the landing
takes place   the device used
to avoid depicting the
actual landing

when years ago I had a similar dream
I remembered it differently

trace of a comma
hovering

series of open parentheses -
flat white plain of cloud
below which we are about to dip

our ability to decry
waiting for a mind
to slip
     each   thing
about it

launch into
pure air
the perimeter paths the
streets take

moving through the city pre-dawn in a cab
when the light comes up colors
wash across a word
    in an explanation of a moment
the failure itself   has some
small lift

STORM SEASON

Several escalations
of sound within
the simple cacophony
of the storm

as ice cores
could tell it if
lifted   into
the light

adding up
    the suggestible road

our portion
of the turning pt.

we do not know what
it is   to itself

flower opening bends
away from the sun
what each limb will
take out
should it come down
      to that   what's been
taken out   to date
in pale storms
of the recent past

somatic tease of
thresholds' blind plank
the strange   token blur
of your focus

outside the home
the cicadas   and the slight
aberrant   breeze

no qualifying heat
before the games begin

DUSK

A letter of disconnect
read in the
snow   falling

light can be said
to be leaving can be
thought   to be closing
around a crowded furlong
of country road

a condition
as it were
of the senses

angulation's re-
purposing a swift grammar
of the outside

dusk's volley   offends
staccato traps enclosing air as
the overcast   darkens to night

JESSICA GRIM is author of *Vexed* (BlazeVox, /Ubu Editions), *Fray* (O Books), *Locale* (Potes & Poets Press), and *The Inveterate Life* (O Books). Recent work has appeared in *The Brooklyn Rail*. With Melanie Neilson she co-founded *Big Allis* (1989-2000), a magazine which emphasized experimental writing by women. A long-form collaboration with Neilson, *The Autobiography of Jean Foos*, is forthcoming in 2025 with Chax Press. She has participated in writing communities in the SF Bay Area, New York, and northeast Ohio. Originally from the Bay Area, she's lived in Ohio since the early 90's, and moved recently to Lakewood.